Terms and Conditions

LEGAL NOTICE

The Publisher has strived to be as accurate and complete as possible in the creation of this report, notwithstanding the fact that he does not warrant or represent at any time that the contents within are accurate due to the rapidly changing nature of the Internet.

While all attempts have been made to verify information provided in this publication, the Publisher assumes no responsibility for errors, omissions, or contrary interpretation of the subject matter herein. Any perceived slights of specific persons, peoples, or organizations are unintentional.

In practical advice books, like anything else in life, there are no guarantees of income made. Readers are cautioned to reply on their own judgment about their individual circumstances to act accordingly.

This book is not intended for use as a source of legal, business, accounting or financial advice. All readers are advised to seek services of competent professionals in legal, business, accounting and finance fields.

You are encouraged to print this book for easy reading.

Table Of Contents

Foreword

Chapter 1:
The Basics Of Running A Business

Chapter 2:
Direct Your Business Towards Your Best Skills

Chapter 3:
Have A Work Area That Is Private

Chapter 4:
Have Good Time Management Skills

Chapter 5:
Use Mentors

Chapter 6:
Stay On Top Of Training

Chapter 7:
Keep On Track Of Promoting

Chapter 8:
Learn To Relax A Bit

Wrapping Up

Foreword

A great deal of people have thought about running a home business once or twice in their life. However, many people have taken those ideas and are actually living them out today, making a living and great profits right from their home. Before starting your own home business there are some things you need to know first. Read on to learn more.

Home Business Success
How To Successfully Run Your Home Based Business

Chapter 1:
The Basics Of Running A Business

Synopsis

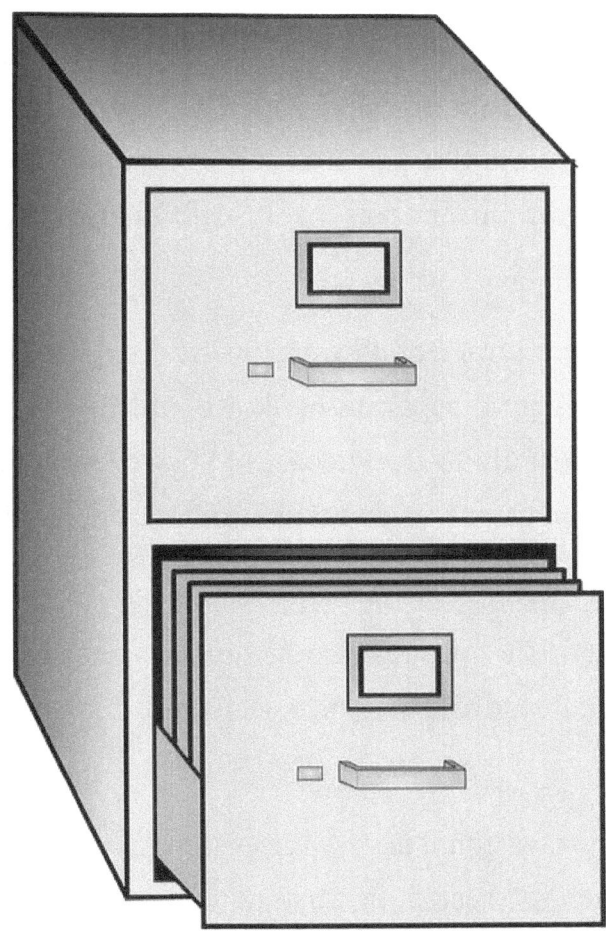

Home Business Basics

Your starting point should be to set up a home office that has a professional feel. This will come in handy to keep you on track as well as motivated, as well if you have clients visiting your office you want them to get a good impression. By doing this you will know when you enter your home office that it is time for work and not time for relaxing around the house.

You also need to take some time to think about what equipment will be needed in order for your business to run properly. These items may include a fax machine, a computer, a printer etc. It is important that you do not cheap out on these tools as it will likely have undesired affects on your business.

It is important that you keep close track of all your business expenses. A great way to do this is to set up a separate bank account for your business. This will greatly contribute to the success of your company. Also, clients who are making payment to you will surely notice your level of professionalism.

The next step you should take is a very important one. You need to create a website and an email address that is specifically for your business.

Trying at all times to appear professional is very important if you wish to gain the respect of others interested in striking up a business relationship or simply being a customer.

Don't forget that your business may require certain files and licenses to be ready. It is important that you acquire these as not doing so can lead to fines or your business being shut down.

These licenses will give the business further accreditation and legitimacy. It will also help to keep the business within the legal perimeters and guidelines designed by various government agencies.

Chapter 2:
Direct Your Business Towards Your Best Skills

Synopsis

Wouldn't you like to do what you love everyday and make a comfortable living off of it? Well dream no more! It is becoming more and more common for people to turn their hobbies and talents into profit generating ways of life. Before quitting your day job, it is important that you do some research on the risk of your potential business first.

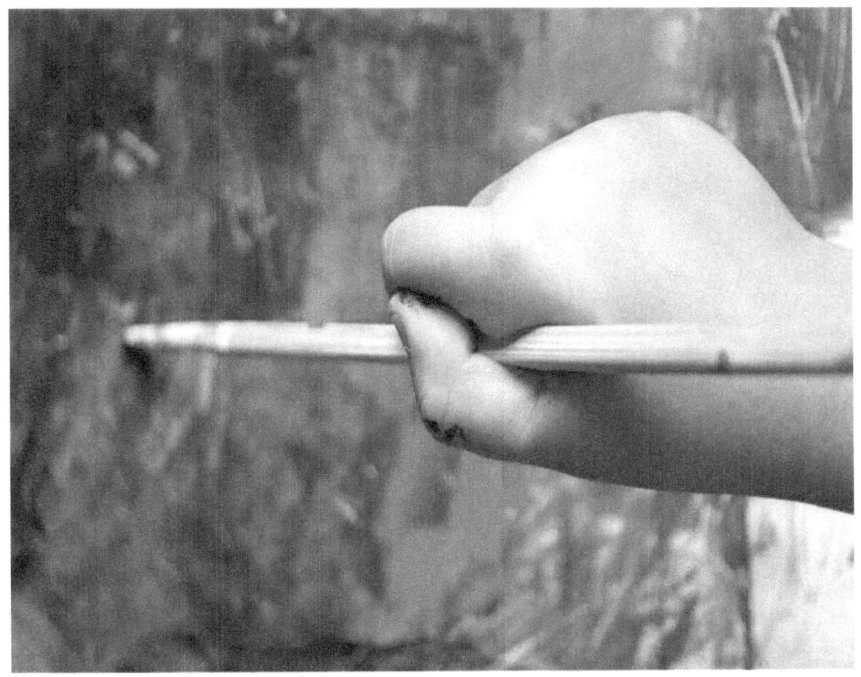

Stick To Your Talents

You should consider the following points when you make this evaluation:

In most cases, an individual who does what they enjoy for work provides much better results with the finished product. This is likely due to the fact that they will not become frustrated, no matter how difficult it is because they take pleasure in what they are doing. Therefore, you should definitely choose to direct your business towards what you enjoy.

Once this business is discovered you need to take time to do some research on how much competition there is. This is a very important step. This will help you to determine how much you will charge for your services and if it will be worth your time. You may end up discovering that you can do something you love to do and get paid for it!

Remember, even though you are at home, it is very important that you incorporate some levels of professionalism in order to ensure success.

Setting up a proper book keeping system, having a list of possible clients as well as creating and designing supporting documents that address the professionalism of the business are all part of the initial set up exercise.

Chapter 3:
Have A Work Area That Is Private

Synopsis

It can be very frustrating when you are trying to complete tasks required for your business and there are distractions going on around you. Therefore, if you are going to start a home business it is very important to provide yourself with a quiet, comfortable and distraction free work area. This area should be private and somewhere you can reach your full potential.

Get Rid OF The Distractions

As you read the following chapter you will learn some key reasons as to why it is so crucial to have a private working area for your home business.

Without a private and professional feeling work area it may be very difficult to get yourself motivated to work. Therefore, it is very important that you do so. The area that you designate as your work area should be solely for that purpose.

When placed in such an environment, an individual will likely fall right into the flow of things. They will be more likely to be productive and reach their maximum potential during their working hours. It will likely also cause the individual to conduct themselves in a manner that is professional and business like.

Having a private working area will also help to keep business related items neat and organized. There is nothing more frustrating than not being able to find something you need for your business. Having a private work area will eliminate this hassle.

Loud noises in the background and other distractions will displease customers and clients. That is just one more added benefit of having a private and quiet working area. time. As well, you will likely be much more relaxed while distraction free.

Chapter 4:
Have Good Time Management Skills

Synopsis

The profit earned by a home business largely depends on the motivational habits of the individual working from home. It is important that they manage their time well and keep on track in order to meet deadlines and keep their business afloat and profitable.

Stay On Track

It can be difficult at times to remain motivated and to stay on track. It is important to meet your deadlines and the following are some tips to help you do this:

Take some time to set up a detailed schedule. This schedule should depict exactly what the individual should be working on and for how long. This is a great way to ensure a business meets its daily quotas.

Each task should have its own time slot. For example there would be a time slot for emails, phone calls, finances and website repairs. Having a specific schedule will keep you on track by ridding confusion on what you should be doing. However, when setting up this schedule it is important to allow yourself a couple time blocks for break time so you do not become overworked.

It is important that this schedule be followed very strictly. If it is not it basically defeats the whole purpose. If you start straying from the schedule you 3will find yourself losing more and more control of your work day.

The success of your business largely depends on its productivity. Therefore, if you find yourself in the habit of procrastinating, sooner or later your business will surely fail.

This schedule will also greatly aid with appointment scheduling. It will not only remind you of the appointment but make sure there is enough time for the appointments set.

Chapter 5:
Use Mentors

Synopsis

It is important to ask for help when you need it. One great place to start is the use of a mentor. Mentors are extremely skilled in their field and their skills can be of great value to your company. Remember, you should never be ashamed to ask for help when it is needed.

Using Mentors

Mentoring is basically an experienced individual who offers their knowledge to help someone with less experience.

The idea behind mentoring is that the mentor's knowledge is supposed to open your eyes to the benefits of your business. Mentors can be helpful in many ways and the following are some examples of how you could put their wisdom to good use:

A mentor can be very beneficial to a beginner with no previous experience who wishes to start a business. These mentors will teach you everything you need to know about a certain topic, adding some valuable insight into the business owners mind.

These mentors will also be able to help you make difficult decisions. Sometimes a decision can make or break a business and this is where a mentor would come in handy. As well, a mentor can be a great place to look for a leg to stand on.

Sometimes the mentoring experience can go beyond just assistance. This is where the mentor can actually embark upon sharing resources and networks with the novice.

This is certainly a huge help to the individual just starting out in the business field. The development possibilities are boundless with this type of extended help and it also helps to eliminate some of the risks the novice would have otherwise taken. Some risks are unavoidable, but with the help of a mentor, the right ones will be taken.

Chapter 6:
Stay On Top Of Training

Synopsis

Falling into the routine of conducting business form home can become quite comfortable. This can be very beneficial but it can also have some undesired results as well. Chances are that if you are comfortable you will not feel the need to try and expand and therefore cut yourself short. That is why it is very important to stay on top of things, especially training.

The Importance Of Training

Staying on top of training is very important. One of the main reasons that it is so important is because it will keep all employees of the business well informed on new tools, practices, innovations and other such advances available in the market today.

Many advancements in technology offer businesses a way to save a lot of time and money. However, if these advancements are to be used, it is important that your staff be properly trained on how to use it.

Setting up periodic training sessions will ensure that you, as well as all of your employees, are on top of modern advancements as well as programs that can help your company succeed.

This is especially important, as most home business entrepreneurs don't have the luxury of being in contact with the cooperate world as a whole, where such changes are apparent and constantly at the forefront for all to be privy to.

Training sessions have many benefits. Not only will you be on top of recent advancement but you may also discover new Ideas and new contacts which will only further the success of your company.

Chapter 7:
Keep On Track Of Promoting

Synopsis

When running a business, it is important to find ways to draw in the target audience. One great way of drawing in people is to use promotions. These promotions will introduce individuals to your product and open their eyes to your services.

Promotions

If you wish to reach out to your target audience and get their attention one of the best ways to do so is to offer promotions. Reaching your target audience is crucial if you wish for your business to be profitable. The success of your business largely depends on the communication efforts of the business as a whole.

As you read on in the following chapter you will discover some important points about using promotions for your business.

Advertising – Although this is a great option it is also somewhat of a costly and time consuming approach. Ads will quickly reveal your business to the general public but if the funds are not available to use this option then forget about it.

Personal selling – being brave and skilled enough to approach anyone and everyone in order to promote the business, product or service is also another way of promoting the individual's company. The personal selling technique is initially initiated through the developing of a relationship with the intended potential customer, which usually evolves into the ultimate goal of actually making a firm sale or commitment on the part of the customer.

Sales promotions – Everyone likes to get extras for no extra cost, which makes this a very affective approach.

Chapter 8:
Learn To Relax A Bit

Synopsis

Stress is something to watch out for while running a business out of your home. It is likely that when tings are not going exactly as they were planned you will become very stressed out. This can be very damaging to your business as someone who is stressed out might make poor decisions. That is why it is extremely important that you know how to relax.

Learn To Wind Down

One of the most important steps in setting up an at home business is designing a schedule. You should make certain that when you make this schedule you allow yourself periodic rest times.

Individuals who are overworked begin to provide a poor quality of work. This makes it essential for the individual to have a break time that allows their mind to relax and rejuvenate, even if it is for a short period of time.

Taking a break does not mean that you have to go on a week long vacation. It simply means that periodically you need to take a few minutes to recollect yourself and ease frustration. You may use this time to exchange ideas with co-workers or possibly even to have small talk.

This in itself is refreshing because it provides the individual with the vital link to the outside world and also connects the individual to all the latest innovations available that may be of help to the business advancement possibilities.

Through this relaxing exercise the individual get to fill up on vital information that he or she may not have been privy to, being stuck at home immersed in the business activities of the day.

Wrapping Up

Don't set yourself up for failure! Working from home may provide certain individuals with a way of making money while being comfortable in the environment of their own home. However, just because you are at home does not mean that there will not be issues that arise. The trick is being prepared for these issues and knowing how to solve them in an effective manner. It is possible and you will surely enjoy being able to make a living from home. I wish you the best of luck and I hope this book was of help!

www.ingramcontent.com/pod-product-compliance
Lightning Source LLC
Chambersburg PA
CBHW030601220526
45463CB00007B/3138